THE EIGHTH MOUNTAIN
POETRY PRIZE

THE EIGHTH MOUNTAIN POETRY PRIZE was established in 1988 in honor of the poets whose words envision and sustain the feminist movement and in recognition of the major role played by women poets in creating the literature of their time. Women worldwide are invited to participate. *The Humming Birds* was selected by Lucille Clifton. Other volumes in the Eighth Mountain Poetry Prize series are:

The Eating Hill
Karen Mitchell
SELECTED BY AUDRE LORDE
$8.95

Fear of Subways
Maureen Seaton
SELECTED BY MARILYN HACKER
$9.95

Cultivating Excess
Lori Anderson
SELECTED BY JUDY GRAHN
$9.95

Between the Sea and Home
Almitra David
SELECTED BY LINDA HOGAN
$10.95

THE HUMMING BIRDS

THE HUMMING BIRDS

Lucinda Roy

THE EIGHTH MOUNTAIN PRESS

PORTLAND · OREGON · 1995

Grateful acknowledgment is made for permission to quote from: "Not the Moon" from *Selected Poems II: Poems Selected and New 1978–1988* by Margaret Atwood, © 1987 by Margaret Atwood. Reprinted by permission of Houghton Mifflin Company, Virago Press, and the author. All rights reserved.

Cover art, *Suffering the Sea Change: Not Venus, but Rising* by Lucinda Roy, used by permission of the artist.

Cover design by Marcia Barrentine

Book design by Ruth Gundle

First American Edition, 1995
2 3 4 5 6 7 8 9
Printed in the United States

The Eighth Mountain Press wishes to express deep gratitude to Adrian Oktenberg who generously contributed financial support for the first five volumes of the Eighth Mountain Poetry Prize.

LIBRARY OF CONGRESS CATALOGING-IN-PUBLICATION DATA
Roy, Lucinda.
    The humming birds / Lucinda Roy. -- 1st American ed.
        p.   cm.
    ISBN 0-933377-39-8 (cloth : alk. paper)
    ISBN 0-933377-38-X (pbk : alk. paper)
    1. Women—Poetry.   I. Title.
PR6068.096H86 1995
811'.54—dc20   95-38457

The Eighth Mountain Press
624 Southeast 29th Avenue
Portland, Oregon 97214
phone: 503/233-3936
fax: 503/233-0774

ACKNOWLEDGMENTS

Some of the poems in this book were previously published as follows:

The American Poetry Review: "Genesis"
Callaloo: "The Votaries" and "Book Review"
Epoch: "Needlework" (1989 winner of the Baxter Hathaway Prize)
Iris: A Journal about Women: "The Word Was with Gods" and "Alice"
New Orleans Review: "Caracole"
Obsidian II: "Lorraine"
River Styx: "The Man Who Played the Trumpet," "Talking to a Writer," "Sierra Leone," and "The Need for Skin"
Shenandoah: "The Bread Man" and "Origami"
So to Speak: "Birth Control," "The Curse," and "The Photograph"

In loving memory of Yvonne Roy, 1926–1992

CONTENTS

I. NARRATIVES IN FLIGHT

II. IN EXTREMIS

I. Narratives in Flight

That's all I want. To be as easy with everything. But I wasn't
born to that. I was born to a time of fire.

—Boy Willie in August Wilson's *The Piano Lesson*

You may believe what I say; for I write only that whereof I
know. I was twenty-one years in that cage of obscene birds.

—Harriet Jacobs, *Incidents in the Life of a Slave Girl*

Yellow Bird

Yellow light pools to crimson;
the headties of women bob up and down like tulips.
The woman pops the scene into her mouth and sucks.

She looks between the white pillars
on her porch and sips tea from bone
china cups imported from England.

The pillars remind her, though on a smaller scale,
of the engraving in her parlor Bible: Samson pulling down
the temple, white pillars falling into fools.

The artist has caught the weight of the pillars—
that's what pulls her, their weight. She hears them crashing
down, another sense entering
the illustration, making it cacophony.

The picture's border is of snakes and roses,
intertwined with titillating symbiosis.
That's what she would have been in another life—
an artist who could make you forget which was which.

Without warning, the niggers take off
into song. She closes her eyes to listen
better. Hot yellow light seeps through her
lids like the long yawn of graves.

Nothing in the world can change while they sing
this strain. She lifts up her arm as if
to capture it. In her mind she sees their song as light—
a great yellow bird glides like an angel across her forehead.
She would paint that too, if she could:

A woman, any woman, all women,
reaching out towards lyricism in the high yellow
light of the afternoon. When Mary appears
to refill her cup, she bats her away. She is in the process
of becoming the yellow bird herself.

What she sees and who she is transpires into shuddering
climax. She lets her legs open beneath her many skirts;
her arms fall to the arms of the chair. The bird is the note
is the song is the flight of her fancy. She blesses her niggers
for taking her where life can be held in the shadows
    of the minor key.

When her only son died last spring,
she wasn't able to lift off from her suffering.
She was tethered like a dog to the table where they laid him.
In her fury, she bit off a hunk of her ring finger, then blamed it
on Mary. The scars are still there. Her own flesh
in her mouth was a diversion.

She had been going mad back then. Yes. For three solid
months she had been mad. She takes a knife
and slits the stomach of the great yellow bird.
She climbs into the cavity and feels what is beating.
She gathers the flesh together behind her like the waists of
    petticoats.
She puts her arms in its wings, fits her
    mouth into the contours of its beak.

Then she is up and over. The ground where he lies
is the diameter of a nickel. She wants to run
to the niggers in the fields and let them know they have
    released her.
But she is limp with triumph; and, as she comes back down
to her station on the porch, her view framed by the white
pillars allows no room for transgression.

Instead she calls Mary, who comes flying out from the interior
and blinks her one remaining eye against the light. As usual
the woman first searches the girl's face: no residue
of vengeance there. Mary's face is a chocolate
bonbon. The woman smiles. "'I have had a rare vision.
I have had a dream, past the wit of man to say what dream
it was. Man is but an ass if he go about to expound this
    dream!'"

Mary bobs a curtsy in reply, then looks down.
"I am not mad," the woman says, still in the mellow grip
of created flight. "I am happy.
Get word out to them to go on singing."
Mary curtsies again and is gone. The woman rubs
the ridged flesh on her left hand where her wedding band
was before the infection.

She thrusts her head back into the chair.
Her eyes are fierce, her mouth squeezed to disfigurement.
Yet—she has not pulled down the pillars. She can see.
Out over the flat plane of her vision salvation
broods against the lemon sky of southern yellow pain.
The walls aren't screaming down.
She is in place above them, hovering like the Holy Ghost.

And, if the great wings cast shadows of melancholy
upon the land where her son lay down in bitter sleep,
these same wings can span the continents of sorrow
inside her and reconstruct the pillar of her soul. She's made
a map to live by. She knows what each line means.
She has solved the riddle and absolved herself from grief.
The niggers keep on singing. She leans back into the wings
of the chair and blesses their simple voices one by one by one.

Needlework

And yes, the view was good
up high upon the block.
She could see between them,
her eyes slipping over the slickness
of their strange hair as they tallied her.
Language is a privilege
so of course she did not speak.
Not then. She saved her store for later
to give to those of her who'd need to hide
in spaces tongues can make.
As a woman, standing on the block
could have been a kind of triumph:
There is wealth in height. And joy.
As a slave, the climbing up was long,
the climb down a closing up.
Later, when she knew that what she'd seen
was where she'd always go,
she bit off a length of thread,
slipped it through a rusty needle and prepared
to sew herself together.
No one would enter her;
no one would leave.
The part of her they prized would fester.
Two months after her sale,
she held the needle up,
its speckled, rusting light
a thin whistle in the dark.
She thought again of home but not in words
because the thinking of them wounded her
and the saying of them burned.
She thought in pictures of the rain she knew

that fell in gashes of caught sunlight
upon those black-green leaves.
She thought of a child. The image of him
hurt her. She turned to thoughts of animals
who, unlike the flaccid beasts
the white folks seeded, knew themselves.
She thought of light and of the one time
she had dived into water here
and had to scramble out faster than breathing
because the light under there was *hers* —a light
she'd left behind was there in water!
So out she flew as if it had been flame
and they laughed, her people,
not knowing where she'd been.
Had the flame from the candle stump
(puckered like a kiss) not died just then,
she would have sewn herself.

She sewed well, they told her, and gave her scraps
of cloth to make their covers with. Joining
their scraps together, she would hum,
weaving strands of song with silence:
From the high palm, the child sees
the beast with lappa ears.
In her heart she follows it.
The earth curves up to where she is.
Together they move.
The earth shakes like the skin of a drum.
The beast passes beneath her.
It is moving as if through water.
It is a great stone. When it stands
Between the suns there is sunset.
The child knows what it is.
So that in the cloth was the invisible
print of an elephant, making the scraps

heavier than their substance.
Underneath the quilt at night,
the white man's wife dreamed
slow monsters, yet was unafraid.
The woman from Africa was moved close
to the big house and taught to sew new things.
She put the fronds of palm trees into petticoats;
they rustled like paper in the sweet Virginia breeze.
She put the child she'd left into the woman's bodice;
it held her tight as suffering
and made her thin. She put tall grasses
into wool and its dullness turned to shimmer
when the sun shone. She put the raw
sienna earth into the shawls she made;
the white man's wife would fancy when she wore it
that her shoulders were wide enough to bear
the eight dead babies that had escaped from her.
They sat upon her shoulders like little white birds.
The white man's woman called her woman "Lucy."
And thought her dull. Four times
she'd have to call before she came:
"Lucy! Lucy! Lucy! *Lucy* !" Then the girl
would fly in like the wind and curtsy,
but the white man's wife could tell
the girl had left a part of her behind in the eye
of the needle. The white man's wife
knew insolence when she saw it.
And yet she also knew
Lucy would lose her babies too,
the ones that slipped from her
in different shades of brown.
No need to punish yet.

                    Lucy's children slipped from her
in different shades of brown (depending
upon circumstance). Trying not to love them
she began to speak with words her mother used.

They knew the calabash and drum,
and though she spoke without a tender emphasis,
love entered on its own to try them.
Time is just the intervals between
the way you look at things.
Now they were drinking her; yesterday
they were gone. She put them in the scraps
with the other one. She threaded needles,
joined them all together in a bombardment,
and sang what it is to know an elephant again.

Things slip. Out. And in between.
There's the outline of a green shadow
a broad banana leaf can make.
A song slips in and out of us like gecko-tongues.
Jazz, blues, gospel, reggae—
the fingers of a hand
that find the clitoris of suffering.
Things slip. Upon a high stage Black is crowned
America. In the light of the tiara
are beads of sun on an old river,
twinkling like parched stars
as the earth heaves upward to become the sky.
Time is just the intervals between the way
you look at things. Now she was taken from the land;
Yesterday I return.
I find her
in the velvet rice fields.
I place her
on thin paths that thread the forest.
She walks. Her toes scoop five places
in pink dust. Her lappa winds itself
around her straightness like a man.
All her babies are her own.

All the cloth she weaves and dyes
have patterns of her own making.
All the making love she makes, she *makes,*
and it is hard to tell how she begins
as it is hard to tell where light begins at noon.
I give her
the limb of a young tree;
she pounds rice to flour in the courtyard of her home.
All the limbs are hers. From grain to powder
rice is hers. The hollow pounding—
out between up and down—
to me is like a mallet coming down
upon chains in the bodies of great ships,
ships with huge clean sails white as pure despair.
To her, the pounding shares the rhythm of the scythe
she uses to behead the grass.
And I am wrong
to think I give her anything.
She is not Lucy anymore. It is not mine
to give or take away.
She allows me passage.
She lets me handle her. She tells me
image is more powerful than substance.
She tells me her name and it is a word
made up of many associations—too numerous
to separate. Although I cannot speak
in words she knows, I have heard the rivers
and the broad leaves. I can remember with precision
the beaks of vultures. I know her name.
Yet for all this, she is human.
She carries gourds on her head
and a boom box in her hand.
She wants red patent-leather shoes.
She wants her daughters to read.
She wants to go to the city to stand and look
through windows at *Bonanza* reruns on TV

as Assieyatu did last year.
She wants to crouch in front with the men
her headscarf scraping the ground of the mosque
her song threading its way up through a gold dome
in prominence to heaven.
She wants to finish birthing.
She is old at twenty-four. Her legs are scarred.
She has seen city women's legs in pantyhose;
she wants it for herself.
She wants no more new wives.
She is tired of accommodation.
She wants to be alone without the weight of a child
on the small of her back.
She never wants to be alone.
She wants to see an elephant. They are almost gone.
She wants a camera and a Mickey Mouse wristwatch.
She wants to be carried to America with a Peace Corps
    volunteer.
She will send for her children later.
She has heard the hum under the earth—
the hum of machines. She knows her land is turned
toward the setting sun waiting for miracles.
She wants one for herself.
She wants to see a plane from the inside,
to fly within its body at great speed
and still breathe. How will her breath
come to her there in the light of the sky?
It will be left behind. She will sail instead.
She has seen the boats once. They are large enough
to ferry all her dreams in.
She will go to America.
She will not go to America. It is too late.
They are not carrying us over anymore.
They have a surplus.
 She pours palm oil from one bowl
to another. There is no deeper orange.

Most of the color we know is the layered kind.
It has a thinness to it, a transparency.
She knows color without an underside—
color like the orange from the palm
brighter than any fluorescent coats we wear
to save ourselves from darks. She pours oil
from one bowl to another. With her finger
she sweeps the remnants from the first bowl
into the fullness of the second. She will take
the second bowl to market, ladling it out,
catching the riot of the day and of the sun
in Coca-Cola bottles. She will hum
while she pours. It will not be our humming;
it will be the hum a drum could make
if it had a subtlety of pitch to match its beating.
She may not know (pouring oil into glass,
her hum winding her world into her mouth
like a fishing line) that she has more
than the patent-leather shoes she saw a woman
wear. When the sun goes down she will be taken
to the movies. Karate kids will leap
across the sewn-together sheets which are the screen.
At every seam their bodies bend a little,
their lethal hands are cupped upon the cloth
to accommodate the thread. The image
even at the point of translation into light
will be distorted.
                    On the road home
I paint her with the fireflies. She is laughing.
Lit insects turn the air to glitter-sky.
From her mouth, it seems, the fire comes,
as if she has made the midnight that she walks in,
the electric swarm around her. In the picture
there is no division between the light and dark.
You see it and forget that night can never be the day.
It is a picture of a thousand thousand suns:

the sun of her mouth as she laughs, the sun
of a million flies; the sun that is moon;
the sun that is the hand-dyed cloth she wears.
And she herself is a part as she is whole—
her outline buried in the bush around her;
her outline firm against the cloth she weaves.
In her room the children sleep against her.
Her song this time is not the song of elephants
or little girls who see the tops of things.
It is the song of growing old and she
would sing it had she not been taken
centuries ago. And it would be like this:
My children sleep around me; the mosquitoes dance.
Always busy with my baby's blood.
Tomorrow we shall die. We shall see
The same my mother's mother saw.
It is little.
The room is smaller than we need,
And hotter.
We work and work.
He chooses me after the new one.
She still tastes fresh to him.
I have my children up against me in my room.
Even in the dark their skin is there.
I see it. The mosquitoes see it too. They dance.
If we should not die tomorrow I shall take
The girls to my mother's village.
She will braid their hair.
She will speak to them of how she braided mine.
They will know me as I shall be,
As I was.
They will know this place is mine.
We shall walk the hill I used to climb,
Look out over wailing grass to find
The greens I used to find when I was young—
When all lands stretched before me

Like my children's shadows do at sunset
When I could leap from mountain top to mountain
And forget the looking down.
They will taste the paw-paw and the orange
And find that they are sweeter from their mother's
Mother's hands. She will make two blankets
From thick thread on a small loom.
All the seams will hold.
My daughters will remind me they are heavy
On the journey home.
I shall tell them,
Carry your blankets. They will be the spirits
You must sleep with
Until you are old.
Just as I have slept with mine.
There is no woman who is not what Lucy
could have been in Africa.

Forever Lucy is at work.
The white man's wife wants four new petticoats.
The lace is virgin white. There can be no blood
on any fluting, no dirt on any pretty curlicue.
Careful. Careful. Sew, sew, sew and back a stitch
and hemline straight, and off the dirty floor—
slap your last remaining child—her pale brown hands
cannot come near the woman's underclothes.
Sew in the fickle, bowing light of the candle.
Sew till midnight and beyond. The perfect cloth
will weigh upon your lap like judgment
as you sew and back and stick and stitch and sew the petticoat
she plans to wear
to church.
The dark opens Lucy
like a tongue. Seduces her. Makes her want

the words she suffocates when daylight comes.
Her fingers move like long black shadows
over snow. They move to the breeze and the drum
like the fronds of palms in a storm that go
with the wind and stay with the tree.
Her fingers move like women.
The white man's wife in her white petticoats
will think of trees in church.
Strange trees with limbs like women's fingers.
When she walks the white man's wife
will see the top of people's heads.
Her feet will be far from the earth,
her head pitched in the sky.
"Make four more by Sunday," she will say.
Lucy's fingers swell. She sews and binds
and oversews a stitch and seams and hems
and prays to gods who are always on vacation.

On Saturday, Lucy's last remaining child is sold.

She does not weep. It was expected.
There are no pale brown hands to slap away
from the white white of the white wife's
pretty petticoats. She does not sew the palms
into the hem. She does not seam a breeze
or thread a purple-green into the needle's eye.
She sings:
From the high palm, the child
sees the beast with lappa ears.
She would put a raging elephant into the cloth
if only she knew how. But all she knows
is what she's always done. She sews
and backs a stitch
and sews the way she has before.
The maid of the white man's wife comes to the door
on Sunday. The petticoats are carried to the house.

Left alone, Lucy does not open shutters.
She sleeps in wands of light
that come through cracks in wood
like the strings of a guitar to stripe her.
She dreams of little girls who hold her hands.
Year in, year out, they never let her go.
She dreams of little girls who carry blankets
from mountain top to mountain. She dreams orange—
of paw-paw and the oil from the palm.
The whole day she is allowed to sleep.
Her work is done. She has been forgotten.
There are no children anymore to wake her
so she dreams them. They are all back home—
the boy she left behind has grown; he is as dark
as beautiful. Her other children pale beside him,
hold his wide hands and call him brother.
Their mother's mother speaks to them.
Even the light-skinned children recognize
the shapes of words she makes. They look around them
and ask her where the fences are. "There are no fences
here," their mother's mother says. They laugh.
Lucy dreams them running in a brown crescent
through the bush. They are naked. No one minds.
"What fine children," her mother says.
And Lucy thinks, "When did all these things
slip from me?" She begins to talk
of petticoats and bodices, underskirts and shawls.
Her mother places one hand gently on her daughter's mouth,
and suddenly the words that Lucy makes are old ones
she thought she had forgotten. And as there is no word
for petticoat or bodice, for underskirt or shawl,
she dissolves them on her tongue like salt
and spits them out, along with a name
she only had for forty years.
                    The voices of her children
swing back to her. She thinks then, "They are mine."

She cannot see the line between the forest
and the children. All of them have arms
like trees and fingers like the fronds of palms
in a small wind.
                        Her mother gives her cloth
to wrap around her hips. And one to tie
the babies to her back. Her mother tells her,
"Wrap the children round you as you used to do."
"They are too big now. Look at them. I have to look
into the midday sun to see them. There are too many."
The mother laughs. "You do not understand," she says.
"The cloth is strong enough. It has no seam."
The old woman calls the children in the dream,
They run across the earth to find her.
She stands them in a row behind the woman who has sewn
a million petticoats. Into herself she wraps them
with the wide and seamless cloth her mother wove. Their feet
rise from the dust. She carries them.
In her ear is the sound of babies breathing;
against her back is the pulse of their hearts;
on her thighs their urgent feet;
round her waist their sleeping hands.

Lucy wakes. Through the shutter cracks
the sun has crawled along her body to her eyes;
the brand of summer rests upon her face.
On the table is a needle and a length of pure white thread.
In the corner is a flour sack of fabric—
the snatchings from the dresses she has made.
She gathers them together, sorts them out
in colors and then counts them.
She has enough. She begins to sew six strands together.
These are hers. The white man's wife
will not approve the seams.
She sews them all together in a long band.

She sews them in a long band and the seams are rough
against her waist as she wraps herself.
The seams are sharp as the groans of the freshly dead.
She unwraps it from her body. She has made it now.
No one else will see it as she sees it.
These are her browns.
She has a right to them.
If it had been their skins she stitched together
she could not have felt it more.
She puts it in a small box—
a box the white man's wife
had kept a feather hat in.
It has a lid. She covers it.
She has recalled them once again
and let them go.
The crickets start their static rush
of limbs. From a high tree comes the steady
fwap, fwap of an elephant's ears swinging
against its ancient, heavy head like sailcloth.

Origami

After freedom came to send the placid cows
whirling through air like figments,

some still hung on to Missy's pretty white head crowned
with curl papers; some to the lopped heads

of black boys stuck up with notes on poles for education;
some to the scorched words on their buttocks;

some to the air they took to,
praying it would buoy them up beyond the paper chains of
   politicians;

and some held hand to silent hand with the beloved
they could choose and the children they could keep.

After the soldier said it, the white rhetoriticians
shut their mouths like guillotines.

The few crazed moments when the world was ass backwards
turned to shreds, floating down to earth again as confetti.

So freedom came to rest the way the dead
do if you don't listen well to their humming.

Soon Missy was calling in the same voice for her sugar
and her tea, her confidante, and her writing paper.

Yet, on occasion, a young black woman or a young black man,
working in the fields with mules, not knowing the war was
   merely Civil,

would look up through gravity to see a flock
of small, defiant birds, shadowless against the high sun.

Gliding through the invisible air,
they signed themselves the aftermath of hoping.

Lighter than parchment and more true,
they urged a path of intricate transgression.

They caught the souls of black girls and black boys
in their beaks to build their fragile nests with.

Cupping their hands to shield their eyes,
the young people stared hard into blindness,

and opened their mouths to the power
of those renegade scraps of artistry

that soared across their vision as only formed things can,
leaving in their wake a mute story, a glory folded up.

The Votaries

Did I tell you about my mammy being a queen? Yes, she was a
queen, and when she told them niggers that she was, they bowed
down to her. She told them not to tell it, and they don't tell, but
when they is out of sight of the white folkses, they bows down to
her and does what she says.
—Ann Parker, formerly enslaved, in *My Folks Don't
Want Me to Talk about Slavery*, edited by Belinda Hurmence

When even queens bled like the others in North Carolina—
it was all she could do to remember there was royalty
under the whorled skin of her mother's back, a crown
beneath the cotton scarf. It is the daughter's story of miracles
that startles us. For how could her mother's people dare
to bow before her, even though the sun was buried in the
   earth
and the small breeze made the grass look like worship?
How could they bear to bend that deep
and listen, even their ears awake in the dust, to a sound
welling up through stones to fondle them?
After her commands how did they adapt to imperatives
bereft of grace? Obey orders that came at them
in the spittle of a man's ragged mouth?
They must have been possessed by some wild idea—
perhaps it began with the way a slave-Queen's head
turned high on its strong brown neck to look at them
and ended with her mouth firm against its own loss.
Perhaps not.
              Either way, they bowed down in the dark
on a plantation in North Carolina
because she told them who she was;
they bowed down,
exhuming the drowned and the raped

and the maimed and the sorry to lay at the feet
of a notion.
And, as they bowed before her
like forgotten words, the Queen must have known
that we claim what we have been
in names that make us so.

The Curse

As red as a tulip, smelling of pots and pans,
my blood announces itself with the clamor of sunrise.
It tells me what I've lost and what I am.
I don't know if those are the same.

In a primary remembrance of pain and intervals,
women bled on slave ships onto the thighs
and cheeks of strangers. The few lucky ones
who expelled their children from them
in fists of retribution felt
their splintered backs pickled in feces and piss
and were glad for their good fortune.

I make these women up.
Except in toilet bowls or garbage,
in birth or times of illness or of death,
I've never seen another woman's blood.
The skin of the egg comes down through me like clockwork.
It has the texture of patience.
I am a woman of color whose son was freely born.

I know nothing.

The Curtsy

The trouble was that Anna's curtsy was a kind of defecation.

Whenever she lowered herself down into the dirt
she took you with her into shit
and left you there.
It wasn't mannerly.
It made pale women light up with fury;
it made ruddy men shift from one leg to the other
as if a slave had caught them
in an act of bestiality.

Even after they lopped off her ears
(Mr. Ellis once or twice recalled they fell to the stable floor
like scarlet petals and lay there for fifteen minutes before the
dogs came in) she still imbued her curtsies with a curse.

Old Ellis decided to let it be.
There was only so much a man could do
to render a woman impotent.
He told his guests she was something of a spitfire
and focused on the biscuits she made—the best
this side of the Mississippi, he boasted.

And after the women left, he'd add:
"These biscuits slip down your throat like the tongue of a
    whore."
And the men would nod, knowing precisely what he meant.

The Humming Birds

At night on deck, when dark reconstructs
his fingers
into the spaces between them, he claps his hands

to sound himself to sanity.
Clap!
From the center of his ship

the sound of two hands clapping
jumps off
into the sea like a skipping stone.

As a sailor, as the captain, he had a sense
of the water's edge,
until the cargo's humming snatched it all away

eighteen nights ago when it took up that note.
He monitors the waves
mercurial in a night encased in vacancy.

The ship shovels a penitence behind her
leaving a shallow trough
in her wake—a mass grave for his dead.

The horizon eases a new world from birth to fugitive.
From below
a female's howls split a womb in half.

His eardrums bleed. He falls upon the deck
and cries out
his mother's name. His body foreshortens into sound.

The captain's ear is everything. A shell. A cave
pinned to the dark.
It becomes a sounding for the news below:

A low hum, shot through with something else—
what is it?
That other, cleaner sound that underscores the humming?

Veils flapping in the wind?
Mouths torn from their moorings,
swinging like gates in the breeze?

A sail caught in a mad gust—
East! West! East! Then West again!
Turning the ship to rocking chair?

Or *wings*?

A thousand thousand African wings
applauding height from the black air
whipping the back of the dark.

The Archangel Michael

He is a man until the leap
when,
in his arc to a net lynched to a rim of steel,
he posits flight as a matter of fact
in a triumph of physical therapy.

Less than a moment,
less than the beat of a heart
or a wing,
he is held up against atrophy—
against the bullet, the steel-toed boot, the lunch
counters, the German
shepherd dogs, Emmett Till and his mother,
the windrush on yellow sails,
the sorrow songs burrowed into cotton,
blues hitting the notes behind the chords of slavery.

Like a taut black banner
he holds our breath for us
and freezes the descent.
And so we rejoice in the finding of two clues:
One.
For us, everything of glory is (somehow) couched in flight.
Two.
It is only the going down that will bring to pass its opposite.

Book Review or
Self-portrait with the Left Hand

I.
The chair is green, the lamp is brass, the floors
are wood, the window open to the birds
where I find my lines. A calm,
provincial setting. Nice. It's easy from here
to sew a lunatic quilt. All I need
are scraps of quiet, then they'll multiply
all by themselves into a larger solitude.
The silence, for example, after the
ejaculations of the hinged niggers
swinging in a smile; the time between the locked
door and the gas crawling into Jewish
lungs like whirling spiders; the moment after
black wings are launched against the air, pitiful
as umbrellas; the peace of femurs, our white
I's on the beds of seas.
                              I can write this
because I am not this, sitting pretty
on a green chair in Virginia, coned by light
from a brass lamp, my feet held to hardwood,
my window open to the sound of flight
and the frantic whir of estrogen.

II.
Lucy takes a needle
And sews her lady's clothes
Her head in plaits of suffering,
Like corn, in rows, in rows.

She sews until her thumb is gone
Her eyes are crossed and blind;
She doesn't sing a sorrow song
Her words are far behind.

Between the coast of Africa
And the Carolina shore
Her alphabet is battened down as language
Turns to door.

When the sea began its rhythm
In her back and in her head
When she knew her eyes were open
To the clamor of the dead.

Lucy takes a needle
And sews her lady's clothes
Her head in pleats of suffering
Like corn—in rows, in rows.

III.
This is my book.
It has my thumbprint on it.
I wear gloves; it makes no difference.
I paint with the left hand and the right—
the strokes are still the same.
I can only see what I can see.
Very well then.
May my thumb be as green as my chair!
May the brass on the lamp that lights me play like a band!
May the floor beneath my feet buoy me up like driftwood!
For I am floating on a sea of flame,
despair flanks me on either side—runway lights.
In this translation from word to flight
and back again,
I will need a strong pair of wings.
I will need, in fact,
to borrow yours.

Suffering the Sea Change:
All My Pretty Ones

What isn't water in us must be bone;
what isn't weeping must be what remains
when weeping's done.
                    Nothing is lost like children.
Those who would have birthed us given time
are singing from their perches on the ocean floor.
They swing to currents and speak to fish.
Their song begins and ends, *Remember me.*

What isn't water in us must be bone;
what isn't weeping must be what remains
when weeping's done.
                    Nothing is lost like children.

Nothing is lost.

Suffering the Sea Change:
Not Venus, but Rising

Flight was a woman rising in time
from the sea. A winged fish, bubbles blistering
the surface as if it were the skin
on a man's back. She rose,
to hang there in the air and wait for them.
Her eyes closed in upon themselves
as she learned twenty million words for cages.
Through a nose broad enough to breathe through,
she took in the air and blew it out again.
She came as a preacher rising up with friends
into all sunsets. She came as a clearing
of the throat between the penultimate breath
and the final exhalation. She came sweet
with pearls in her hands and the print of wings
on her forehead. Her shadow was cast
in scales. Her shadow was a great fish
flat enough to skip across a body of water
on the way back home. *Back home* was there
in the Benin contours of her face, and the eyes blank
as any target. Not expressionless, just beyond
expression where depths collide and no one
remembers which word goes with which dark.

They saw her—the kidnapped. They looked down
at their feet and felt their weight.
They looked up. She was there. They looked down
again and waited for something
to break.

The Man Who Played the Trumpet

As usual, he began with steps. Their steps.
He wound them down from his lips
like rope ladders, teased and flirted,
said it could be this way
could be that, made them almost breathe
the note themselves, the note he wouldn't touch.
Then he took them up like skylines,
like pity, like storylines,
like pearl earrings strung on kites,
like wine as red as sound blown out round
through trumpet brass. The people forgot
who they were. They forgot
what they were. They forgot
how and why and when they were
seduced into sound.
Holding their lips apart as if to receive communion,
their torsos leaned into the hollows
he made for weariness to lie in.
He took them down, up, and back
like a dance partner. Down, up, and back.
Down, down, up, ba-ba-back, and back—
not to a remembered place, but to a place
where forgetting was the only clean thing to do.
He took the band with him too.
They rose and their arms and hands
urged them on to the crucial point,
yes, the crucial point, where what was felt
was what was played, and there was at last,
at last, no gap between the feeling
and the knowing and the being there.
They saw the glare of the bright

original circle. His people got up
in their shadows, let their bodies go,
and stepped out into his trumpet
as if it were a back door—
as if they were his lost notes going back
to find the desire that made them.
If they could have spoken, perhaps
they would have said it was like dying
or like being born, when what is about to happen
is a frame inside which everything
you must do comes to pass.
Beginning and end welded together:
retrieval and loss, play and pause,
dance and stasis, essence and imagery,
rhythm and silence, effect and cause,
and life! And life! And *Life!*

The Virginia Reel

In nineteen ninety-four, the plantation
hums with tourists; the slave quarters are full
of whimsy. It is fall. The leaves are scarlet.
The guide points out the cabins as they lean
into winter. He whips us into frenzy—
the banquets, the gardens, the cooks, the maids,
the butlers, the grandeur, the books, the balls—
always the balls. Women dancing like girls,
in corsets tight as fists; men, heady with
perfume, ready to die for a kiss.
Outside the trees are on fire. It is fall.
Inside the enormous house a staircase
defies the laws of gravity, suspended
from the landing like a Bible vision.
We say half-jokingly it cannot hold us.
It does, in spite of logic. We talk
about the years it took to build those stairs.
Our guide is close to tears as he caresses
smooth brown wood.
We hold on to the railing. We could fall,
all of us together, if the structure
doesn't hold. We climb. It holds. We shake
our heads and laugh. Laughter takes us
into double-barreled spirals, a falling
into where we were before.

                          It is fall
and hoops and petticoats sweep the master's house,
and Lucy carries the mistress' chamber pot
softly down the stairs. Rawhide shoes
(greased with tallow so they slip right on)

make the workers quiet. Yesterday a man
stood up and flew home.
Mary witnessed it, so did Rebecca,
Hester, and Prince Josiah. Not like birds,
they say, but like leaves raised up by whirlwinds,
Elijah the Fool flew on home. Too dumb
to grow wings, Hester says, the poor fool screamed
and tried to cling to her headtie. But no one cheats
the Lord. Elijah stole her red headtie.
Hester wants it back. In the fields, dreaming
is dangerous. Hester is whipped for staring
at a cardinal. "Birds is birds," the foreman
says to her. That night they gather in a flock
of hope and stand where the Fool had stood. Nothing.
No one remembers the words that brought them
here. Elijah knew them. Hummed
the songs he had the words to. Never shared
a damn thing. But catch him unawares and hear
something wild coming from his throat. The same
sound he made when the whirlwind took him up
and spun him round like cotton on a spool and
flung him up into the sky above their heads.
Elijah's clothes tore off his back, his shirt
waved to them before it fluttered down.
Prince Josiah wears it now and stands there
in the spot where foolery had stood and nothing happens.
Mary blinks her one remaining eye
in the dark and thinks she hears a sound
like white folks' clothes swishing up the leaves.
"Ghosts!" she cries and scurries into dark
with all the rest. Lucy thinks about the Fool.
Up in the air it is quiet. She knows
the tops of trees. Brought late into this world,
she still recalls the other. She has brown scraps
sewn together in a band to match
her stolen children's skins. She knows water

in a river and the green of leaves
a deeper green than southern green; and she
remembers names for places and names for friends
and names for when they took her out of breathing
into wood. She mumbles something close
to prayer, holding the chamber pot away
from her skirt as she winds down the spiral
staircase. He flew! She will conjure up words
again, and see if she can call the wind
the way Elijah did, wrap it round
her body like a coat, and fly back
to the light of ancient rivers. In the wake
of flight, she hums songs taught her by her
mother's mothers.

              The music room is oval
like an egg. The guide points out the rounded
hearths and mantels; curved glass echoes the mistress'
harp and violin. "Harmony," he says,
"the great quest for harmony lives in the walls
of this house." People nod. (Beneath the stairs
the swish of muck in chamber pots and Lucy's
hum, suspended in the sweet Virginia breeze,
riding the updraft of air like flame.)

II. In Extremis

We need to be each other's names and what we are
asking. Do not be anything. Be the light we see by.

—Margaret Atwood, "Not the Moon"

In Extremis

My mother had the sense to see it:
When trees howled
and onions sobbed like wives,
when the earth shivered
in its own sweat
and people twined about
in ecstasy, she kept her eyes open
and her ears pinned to the ground.

She was rarely prudent;
never circumspect.
She gazed into breadth
and made it taller.
Addicted to the coy blossoming
of a world hard and full as a nut,
she searched for the white screams
of epiphanies.
She sat next to the void
with *Wuthering Heights* wide open
on her lap
and didn't tremble.
While *Carmina Burana* blasted holes
in her chest, she listened,
her eyes open,
her hands out in front, vulnerable,
as if her heart
were a breakfast tray.

That was my mother.
No different from other girls' mothers
at first glance—

but put her inside trees
or balance her on books,
sit her on top of Salisbury Cathedral
or ask her a question about the depth
of my father's grave,
and she'd make the vertical journey again.
To spire or tomb, it didn't matter.
What counted was the setting out.
And her willingness to make the trip.

The last time,
I knew what the journey cost her.

Now for the hard part—
to find precisely where it was
she went.

Cancer

All were convinced that the world would end when the planets moved into line with each other in the constellation of the Crab.
—Barbara Walker, *The Women's Dictionary of Symbols and Sacred Objects*

1. *December*

The crab moves quickly.
The claws are tenacious.
You hold on against all signs
and interpret yourself as usual.

2. *February*

The doctors are amazed.
You've beaten them.
The crab aligns himself
and gets to work.

3. *May*

Caught in the agony of claws,
you turn yellow as fall,
bloat with fluid, begin
the process of drowning.
He has you.
He's pulling you down.
The planets have moved.
The world ends
in increments.

4. *June*

I fly to England to say good-bye.
Everything in London needs cleaning.
You are embarrassed.

5. *Ever After*

I turn you into a water rose.
You, the rose, stay fresh under the dirt
like a cluster of white, scented stars,
or a group of virginal cysts
always multiplying, always vivid,
always, Mother, benign.

Sierra Leone

It's the palm trees I remember—
as languid as the underwater braids of Indian girls;
and the morning, swiping the night away like a loaded
tablecloth in one magician's gesture;
and the paw-paws' ruddy orange flesh and tender
succulence; and the way the rain unfurls
the earth; and the imploded
songs of birds popping the air like bubbles; and the pressure
to know it all by heart by sunset.

The point is I am living
in Virginia now with your shipped belongings
and a sentence full of exclamation points.
You were with me for a few weeks, there, in the first stanza,
before they buried you in one magician's gesture
and I learned by heart the things that children learn:
You are dead. You came to visit me in Africa.
You were my friend, my mother on the side. You died
in flesh as yellow as the yokes of eggs, the grotesque
bubble of your liver imploding like a
circus trick,
your sparse hair languishing under therapy.

The point is I can see the palm trees.
Again and again, I see them.
You are there, pointing out the birds,
your face lit up as if by magic, your face unfurled
to the pressures of the air, while you take to heart
the words of one song only:
And it is dying.
And there is no refrain.

Penultimate Rites

Since my mother's death,
      life consists of gaps and tabulations.

The space is for the words she would have spoken;
      the indentation
for the width
      of my replies.

Stained Glass

He's dead.
His head hangs
lyrically to one side;
his fingers cup around the brutal nails
as if they were small birds.
Beside the cross the women weep like thunder—
the men prepare to hide.

Light makes the glass an oxymoron:
mournful optimism and brilliant dark.
The people come in flocks
to see the show of light. The altar
is flecked with his blood, neon-red
in the journey from glass to stone. The psalter
is pressed to the lectern by the sheer force
of color, blasting through the high window
like alleluias.

For the ones with faith, like my mother,
pews rise into the pictureglass.
The chosen are with Mary, gazing up
into the wide mouth
of pain.
The window makes something happen.
They see him there. In flesh, in blood.
They will be saved; there's no redeeming them—
the faithful ones who have no need to ask who moved the
    stone.

Flying Buttresses

My spirit is unruly in the paradox of flying stone.
In places like this, I wear my mother's face;
it contracts under pressure from angels and edicts.
I enter the stone; the stained light
of nave and chancel diffuses me.

Marble is passion quenched in stone—
a balance between sentience and numbness.
Kneel.
It is cold enough.

The spire sways to high-strung incantations,
and the candles grope toward the dark.
Incense laces the air like a madrigal
and the wood pews carry the scent
of coffinmakers.

Like my mother I am attracted to death
when it is forced to stand still and endure.
My mother knew where to go in a cathedral.
She headed straight for the tombs, then walked over
to the candles and lit one as I do now.

In her coffin a slim lick of light
defines the dark.

Surfacing

Winter light accommodates the pallor of the dead.
February has a yellow cast and a grave
consistency.
When I paint it I will leave out
shadows to bring death to the surface.
The picture will be too sorrowful. I will hang
it in a closet in the dark.

My mother is one of the yellow dead.
We buried her in a double-depth grave on top
of my father eight months ago. By *yellow* I mean
aged, like cheddar or parchment, teeth or someone's
fingernails. In the cemetery where she took root
the cypress trees are taller than a French Impressionist's
whimsy. There is a rose garden to her left
across the driveway. If she sits up
and cranes her neck she'll see the blooms.
Perhaps to her they'll look like long-stemmed kissing.

I can't believe in absolutes. I like conditionals—
the ifs and buts and whens that make for relative grief.

My son is singing his favorite song:
"I'm a baby, gotta love me,
big purple eyes and very cuddally...."
His voice isn't porous; it's a brass band.
I grab hold of him and plant him in front of me.
We are oblong in the mirror. He is as big as I am.
We look at ourselves and laugh. Same dimples,
similar hair. Our teeth are white. Age cannot touch us.
If we were a picture I'd painted

there would be pale yellow signatures across our faces.
But no one has painted us.
We occur without mechanics.
I do not make everything happen.

My mother sits up to look.

For My Son

When I die, whatever form I take will be close
to song. When you part the grass ahead of you
like hair, you'll feel the undertow of harmony
pulling at the soles of your feet, and your journey
will be made glad.

When you call out in the complex dark, your voice
will come back to you as mine,
and dark will be made simple again.

If you stand on the gentle mound of my grave
and listen to the earth, you will wonder
what death has to do with breathing.

And if you dream of wings working a sweet hum
from the air, my son, they will be mine—
ready to carry you and your loved ones home,

ready to carry you home.

Making Love

Your dresser mirror sang to us of holy water
as sweat and sheets and grace and hands and feet
made hummingbirds of bone.

                    This, my friend,
is love. This frenzied, beating lapse into
the white curve. In your room, love
held me like a pennant in the frantic air,
and we rose together down
accompanied by the valiant descant of your
dresser and your bed. Two people in a
small boat spinning the navel of the world.

Nothing will not change now that this has been.
In the wings between your shoulder blades
I find the thing omitted from the argument
and unravel it, trembling, like a metaphysical conceit.

The tongues say *aye* and *aye* again, and no one
turns a head to glance behind.

                    This, my love,
is friendship. Take it. While your mouth is
open,
mine will play its part.

                    Look! The sky, too,
is open as a gate. Stiff in the holy
seizure it walks through us. We do nothing
but feel the hymns of the stratosphere hinged
to our parts like gods.

Sexuality

When love is good it impersonates the ritual of rain,
rhyming itself over and over in refrains
of quenching. Not even the intellect can halt it.

The body in love builds upon the wasting flesh
a counterpoint to mystery when the fresh
touch of prime love hoists the sky to tiptoe.

Then we are real again—as real as eggs,
and more tightly packed against the dregs
of day, waiting for the night to come and open us;

as flowers open too with a protein scent;
and electric color schemes shock pupils meant to be content
with the lint of glory. Two gorgeous balloons

swelled into thin, expansive sensuality.
This is love making its repeat debut. An actuality
of what cannot be there—a vision soldered onto skin.

Talking to a Writer

O, she said, if only we were virgins!
Mountains would arch beneath us like the vertebrae of cats,
our mouths would reveal our tongues, naked as peeled
bananas, and the sweet museum of our sheets
would convene delight!

I have written of a similar phenomenon, he said
but the notion of the virgin and the mountain and the cats,
the mouths, the tongues, the naked fruit, the mausoleum
sheets inspires me. I'll let it settle—sherbet on the tongue,
then pause before reciting.

O, she said again, her voice a staircase lower.
I think, she stumbled to a word, I think I'm...disappointed.

I can't see why, he said. You knew I slept with books.

But you changed my sweet museum to a mausoleum.

Christ, he said, yanking on an argyle sweater, battling with
a sock. Museum! Mausoleum! What's the difference?
In the widening circles of slammed doors she replied, I am.

Sustenance

When we made love your eyes were always open
to interpretation.

We traveled to the far rim of the wide plate of ecstasy
to eat, leaving no trail of crumbs behind us.

Now, the half-moons in my toenails ache;
the follicles of my hair are weeping.

The objects you left me are indelicate as pain.
The earth is flat.

The lovely shell you snatched from the sea as a gift
whirls toward its center—empty as a room.

Untitled

Today I have been hurled out of the story of my life.
I stood at the window and watched me go in fractions.

My narrative passed me by with the resonance of taxi cabs.

Today you will never love me again. I get the point at last.
I am quiet. The place for agony is the tomb or the file drawer.

Romance has a period at the end; and on the hills
evergreens are dotted like toilet brushes.

Although I feel as though we've forgotten something—
a glove, or an umbrella, or a snippet of evidence,
I understand why you have to leave.

When all gestures serve to incriminate,
nothing is worth the going back.

Triple Overtime

I don't know what the final buzzer means.
My journey takes me by storm. I arrive
at the wrong place three days too late wearing used clothes
and someone else's underwear. I seem to be wedged into
   intervals:
the sharps and flats of absurdist closure. I want to know
how to get there on time. I want to be able to predict turns
and resolutions, but ellipses siphon one fear into another—
dot curve, dot dot curve—the morse code of an antipoet.

They tell me denouement exists. There's a plateau after pain,
   they say,
Emily knew it, so did Shakespeare. Maybe it's a white thing.
But no! For here is Hubie Brown talking to my man Robinson,
the Bud Light player of the game. Following a trinity of
   stalemates
he's performed his miracles again.
Hubie, speaking for the common folk, reassures us
it can be done, simply, abidingly

because it was.

Divorce: The Old Sestina

The builder says I need a new roof—
Soon. The old one is buckling. Tiles curl
up like stale pepperoni. The woman
I used to be never flagged. She could laugh
at broken things, then mend them with a finger
dipped in Christmas. She was lucky.

When my son was born I tasted lucky.
Luck crunched up against your teeth like hail on a roof
and gave me power. On my ring finger
was gold enough for sleeping in a tight curl
around a man. Our bed would laugh
with us. You a hold-back man; me, a held-in woman.

There is no such thing as the other woman.
If there were, I would thank my lucky
stars for precise enemies. My laugh
would tumble upwards in a spiral to the roof
then through the chimney down again to curl
around my spine like a bandage round a finger.

I remember all the animal moves your finger
made and there's the rub. A woman
has so many places for a hand to flex and curl
inside. You found them all. I was lucky.
So, I hope, were you. With you in the roof
of my mouth, even my fillings laugh.

On Tuesday I will set aside a time to laugh
at risible angels giving me the finger
while I climb up nonsense stairs to a sheer-drop roof

where I was meant to go, being woman.
Coming down I smile the usual children's lie—for *lucky*
is a word I must wind upon his forehead like a curl

or curse. My love never curled
up round the edges like a grin
or a grimace. Blind dumb luck
drove me to you. Luck was the finger
pointing the way to life as a good woman
who draws light from dead coals, turns grey slate to candy on
  a roof.

I curled your long sweet fingers
into my laughing mouth from baby-time to womanhood
as we built the unlucky roof, Velcroed to small heavens.

The Ride

My horse has wings.
The flight from purgatory
is a kind of suicide. Self becomes a thin line
mounted on the back of speed.

My horse gathers and leaps
like a metaphor.
Flank and neck and hoof and rump willing to extend
to the beat of wings. Speed multiplied by grace.

My horse has wings.
In the round well of her eye are skulls
and evolutions. She lets me ride
without asking whether I am worthy of the gift.

She is the only one who does this.
The sky is mute when we ride, but the earth is louder
than canon fire, and the air is torn
in half, and from somewhere comes a sublimity of water.

Suddenly a section of the roof of the world collapses
under the strain. She and I—
friends—burst through the cavity
like flame.

The Key

I've lost too many times to count, but I've
      won the little faith I use to bear the loss.
You say *love me,* as if such a thing were
      still a possibility
If it is, it's a tiny door on the other side
      of a ragweed path to bitterness.
And if you reach the door you'll find
      it locked and overgrown with moss.
For all your chopping and your declarations
      it will hold.

I'm sour now, sour as old milk.
      I don't have time for violins or the puerile naughtiness
of sin, or the wide grins of ecstasy or for passion
      that causes whiplash or the fifty-yard dash
toward the rapid pulse or the silly groping
      of those who should repulse. You do, however,
fascinate a little. And it may be that there may be
      a key you could borrow
for a week or maybe three. A tiny sweetness
      left in me—congealed and hard, it's true—
a chip off someone else's candy.
      But you may have it, if you dare.
There.
      It's yours.
            The key to me.

Go on.

Lick it.

Iris

The petals are tongues, not beards,
    crimped at the edge, like pastry.
These flowers are voluptuous
    on their long, straight stems.
The form the iris takes demonstrates
    the connection between blossoming
and intimacy. These flowers make me laugh.
    They are like women.
They are not afraid of opening wide.
    Inside is a yellow flame and color, color, color
falling out from the center like water
    caught in light. Look at them.

This is how you should make love to me.

The Need for Skin

The moon sweats
and the night is dense, black grass.

The moon sweats into climax,
and the night is triggered with gunpowder blue.

The moon is vibrant with mouths;
I pull them open and listen carefully against the silence.

If it is to be endured, everything
must either laugh or weep.

So love me with all your mouths open. And let the lonely
O's echo off the caves of our skin.

If we make mirrors of the world,
there is nothing to be afraid of.

We two are the moons—both of us substance and shadow;
reflecting the depth of the sky.

The Heretic

What has radius beyond all talk
of circles is the moon.
White in an effect of substance,
she wears her own sweet collar as a halo

and tells us how to hear in tongues.
Between her ebbing mechanisms
what is water in us subjugates
to the premise of her shafts.

I talk to the sexton moon
and wish her well. She knows me.
Her mouth opens to my neck;
she clings like white tar.

I enter her wide vowel like an embryo.
In the silver waterlight the litany begins
as the Usual God of Torque and Talk is shackled to the dark
by the incalescent aves of my moon.

III. Women (in)Form

Theirs was not a tender, compassionate, romantic world.
And yet in a way it was.

—Bessie Head, *The Collector of Treasures*

To know all truths approximate, dependent on a sum of
knowledge in constant flux; to accept all situations as
unstable, and nothing constant but change....

—Lao Tze

Caracole

In my garden, by the planted vegetables,
the snail's back carries the curve of the world;
the patterns on babies' heads; Yeats' causal

stairway; a million other claims for what we see....
She knows, this snail—her worm body inside
secrets, signs, all appropriated—how she is, most utterly, a
    snail.

Yet I have learned something:
that a thing is as far removed from its symbol
as a snail's inedible shell is from its tender succulence.

In my garden, the snails dance snotty networks
across the crazy paving. On a good day, I twirl with them
up and over, round and up, into the buried stars.

We have spent our centuries looking for the door at the top
of the stairway, imposing manifestation on simplicities,
making our words reverse back onto themselves with deeper
    meaning.

We have made the snail dance. Really, she is sluggish.
Underneath the broad leaves of tomatoes, by heady cucum-
    bers,
ghastly squash, in slower motion, she squats and squats and
    squats.

Years ago, my mother's tortoise, Albert, was bombed
in London's Blitz. Shrapnel in his shell, the old campaigner
inched along through peace without complaint. My mother's
   eyes well

when she speaks of this absurdity. Before I knew
the fragility of all shells, I used to laugh.
A shell-shocked tortoise! A thing of little worth.

Now it seems to me (and please don't laugh)
as though the hump of his tiny paving stones
pitted with fragments of war is a part of that crazy dance

of other shells. Not that, in some way, we are all Albert,
pitted and crawling back into the earth, victims
of other people's wars. No. Too crude.

But finding the whorls of snails around the things we eat,
remembering the backs of tortoises in the slabs
of stones that lead me from my house down to the street,

there is a sense of how abstraction limits itself to symbol
if we let it. And all I can offer now is resistance
to created myth, and sign, and metaphor. All I can do

is join the spiralling dance to nowhere,
step on things that break as easily as we allow them to
in yards where all extraordinary drama is played
out in half turns to the right and to the left, then lost.

Famine

While the dogs I'd seen at noon lying in the road,
their eyes flat, their tongues hopeless with abiding thirst,
howled across the town at night, women gave birth
with the regularity of famine
and buried their children
beloved in the futile earth.

They prayed to an African sky fraught
with coy wishing stars and the lopsided grin
of somebody's hard white mouth.

The same story rolled itself over
and scratched the sores of the town;
and the women joined with the call—
chastising the hunt,
chastising the obese pearl of the moon.

The Bread Man

Bread-oh, bread-oh, ten-cent bread....
It reaches me in a finer consistency
sifted with the sunset, as if
the sun and he are different ends
of the same note—as if
they've strung a line between
them from which time
is hung.

I don't know how to write
about absolute stillness
when words themselves disrupt the surface.
The breadman's call is the perfect dive.
Nothing seems to shift for it—
nothing is agitated. Forty loaves
are balanced on his head.
He walks from Masingbe to Mondema
without shoes.
In the Northern, the Eastern, the Southern
and Western Province his call is the same:
Bread-oh, bread-oh, ten-cent bread.
He reaches up and fishes for a loaf,
careful not to incline his head too much.
He hands her the bread; she hands him the money.
It is a gesture full of meat.
Both know how long it took
to get them to this point of brief exchange.
He moves on into his call,
walks barefoot
into the notes he sings.
leaving his signature upon the dusk—calligraphy.

Genesis

I don't know where things come from anymore.

I used to know when I lived in Africa
and bananas grew in my backyard
like the penises of wild green men;
and the scent was as heavy as Del Monte
on the pineapple farm, and white chickens
squawked in the patient hands of executioners;
and the sun swelled in the East at the appointed time
and dissolved in the West according to schedule.

In America, nothing comes from anywhere.
I say again, the fruit is divorced from the tree,
and I have no idea how the men in the moon
got back, or how anchormen are pistoned
through the atmosphere in particles, or what machine
endowed my offspring's vitamin with a Flintstone,
or where else those chops have been
en route to freezer burn.

The great myth has always been origination.
Now it is origination once removed.

When we find the first seed
it will be covered in Saran wrap
and laid to rest in the shrine of the Light
of Fluorescence.
When people come to make obeisance,
no one will remember how to get back
to prayer.

The Photograph

Three years later the small scar
on her left arm and the bunched flesh far
up beside the inside place is all she has
to remember the visitor by, whose name
has never softened on her tongue, but flames
there like vivid yellow graffiti to reclaim her
when she least expects it to.

Three years later she is thirty-five.
The small pencil scar still on her left arm,
the bouquet of flesh alarms her
gynecologist, until the tricky things he did
with the soda can bring enlightenment.
Her doctor says, "At least it's nothing
nasty, then," peeling off his rubber gloves like skin.

The skin around his throat was loose,
and sometimes, if the fancy takes her,
she imagines he stored things there,
spitting them out between his even teeth like bullets.
He kept his mother there, she thinks, and his father too,
and the swelled red tongue and cracked mirrors
he hurled into her face, and a throat coated in obscene despair.

His despair she carries with her on her back,
and in the small and vital space between her legs
where the mound of scars clusters like hard grapes.
Three years later, a part of her still belongs to him
and to January 4th, from 10 to 2, when the moon
was a white scimitar through lace curtains, and the pretty
knickknacks in her room mocked her with inconsequence

and the phone rang twice—both times
her mother who left late New Year's messages
on the answering machine, which is, perhaps, the fulcrum
of her suffering because now her mother's voice is inside
her with the man's tongue and it's hard
(Jesus, it's hard) to remember sounds before
they were lodged inside like shrapnel.

So today she's sorting through the photos to find the one
where they are together under the oak—she and her mother—
their arms out like tree limbs waving the still air like fools.
If she finds that picture and can click back to the high laughter
of two plaited voices, she will feel the bunch of roses
up beside the inside place and see the small
scar on her left arm and not be appalled.

Maybe. So she looks for it with a necessary vengeance—
her fingers sorting through memory to find a nail
on which to hang futility and let it rot.

She finds the picture. It is not as she remembered.
It is smaller: Her mother's matchstick arms
are raised above her head; the child is doubled over aching
with the pain of laughing, oblivious to her brother's camera.
Happy, happy, happy,
with her mother being a tree
in some corny photograph.

When her mother calls the way she does each evening,
some time after 10, they talk,
as the moon slips in among the stars,
just like itself, snatching the night away
from imagery. Drawing back
the lace, the woman stares into the night.
It is bare; it is hers; she must keep it.

What Is Dangerous Not to Remember

We learn pain. It abides between our shoulders
at the base of the neck in the old pivot of wings we've lost.
Better then not to listen to flight whose sounds can damage us.
Better to love blue as a color not a point of view.
Better to be a cow in a field, cloven hooves stuck to the earth,
tongues fat with cud. Better to let the swan
draw physics from desire and mount the air
in a blizzard of white.
Better if there were not men with a taste for steak
and an acute skill with knives.

Cat's Cradle, Hopscotch, and Jumprope with Priscilla Bean

Hinged to puberty, we city girls
make cradles for our cats
to lie in.
Our are fingers thick
with play.
On the ground between our legs
we number honest squares
to hop in.
A rope swung between us
like a smile spans a place
of leaping
into calculated risk.

Dusk recedes like a hairline.
We three colored girls—me, my sister
and Priscilla Bean—
number our squares in the dark,
wind string around our fingers
and turn smiles upside down.

Priscilla's leaps are timely. Already
she has learned what *careful* means.
She anticipates the rope
and steps beyond into the radius
of safety.
It's hard to trip her up
however fast we turn.
But we do it in the end.

A game works only when you're witness
to the point of loss.

We've learned positioning is everything:
We Three Girls
jumping up against the dark
to the only city song
that ever kept
its word.

Women in Form

1.

Carmen

When Carmen sings, the world takes off its clothes
and people think of flesh and fingers twitch
on thighs and men swallow hard and think rich,
as if thinking were enough to heal their woes.
When Carmen sings, the dark stands on tiptoe
and melodies lie flat and warm against the pitch
of her black notes; and Ed thinks she's a witch
because her black eyes always seem to know
where he's been. Carmen sings notes that would sever
you, and looks out past the edge. She puts words
in your mouth the way a man inserts his tongue
and you mistake what's heard for touch, so feathers
are what you listen to—a flock of birds,
silhouettes of grief against this woman's song.

2.

Alice

is having a baby tomorrow. The kitchen
calendar is circled. Scheduled for a C-section,
Alice is perturbed by the itineraries
of motherhood. She knows the preliminaries
will be easy: Roger will be there, her doctor,
her insurance company…but what shocks her
is her lack of feeling. *She wants something
to happen*--she wants to break down while driving
through Arkansas' Ozarks. She wants to give birth
in a forest, her wetness and the wet earth
two things to taste together like salt and semen.

It won't happen. She is Alice. A pillar
of strength and prudence. Tomorrow they will bill her
for the scar, and she will thank them kindly for her baby,
   Freeman.

3.

Lorraine

is a prostitute. Gentlemen take her
for very little. She waits on Primrose Hill,
a fantasy for the right man. She killed
someone once in an alley after he'd filled
her with spit and knocked out five of her teeth. The
   shrill,
hormonal call of the moon isn't in her.
She fakes it for money. Lorraine is cold
in spandex, but she shimmers like a circus,
and her black skin resonates like a minor
chord. At fifteen she has the finer
points of loving down pat. Tonight the curse
has got her, but her purse is empty. She folds
her hands like an old nun and waits in the necessary gloom
of the Primrose. A sweet child under a glib slip of a moon.

4.

Fatmata

Matron saw it first: the round belly full
of someone's sin. She ran to tell the Mother
who stood and watched her pupil in the shower
stall with tight lips and a beating heart.

The shock came after the expulsion
when her civic-minded father brought her back
at the end of a rope like a mule.
All the nuns could feel was a repulsion
for the man dragging his child to the seat of power
and presenting her like a coarse, deflowered
village maid. Mother Mary claimed he was a fool
to parade his lapse in public like some tart.
She never used those words of course—she was Catholic.
She wept and placed a hand upon her voodoo crucifix.

Birth Control

She is pregnant again. The child pushes out in front
of her in exclamation points.
Poverty is the trip to the
clinic six months
after the blood
has stopped
being explicit;
it's the impertinence
of white social workers
who told you not to do it again
and there you are, large as a cow and twice as costly.

Wealth is the small, crinkled forehead and the mammalian
mouth, frenzied, as if, after all, you are a thing of significance.

Custodian

Twelve men sit around a table. Something else
in the center. Enter the room and assume
there's only a dozen—the centered female
is the table, her face brown and angular, her complexion
fingerprinted like the effect of age rings on the hearts of trees.
The woman is not talking. There is laughter in the room.
It hangs there like a crucifix.
The door opens. A cue. They take it,
brush off the crumbs
And leave.

The woman in the table leaves too, I think.
But you can't tell for certain.
The way a slab of sun slants across the wood
makes me wonder what light means,
which brings me to the dark and the woman's eyes
like the sound of great bells ringing
in towers. Behind all this in the negative space of the painting
is a motion—it could be the breeze in a single olive tree;
or the final exhalations of a young man
with extravagant parentage;
or the sound of one woman bending over to sweep
the floor: swish-SWish, swish-SWish
with a broom or her hand or her hair.

The Word Was with Gods

In fact, there were two gods who witnessed in six days
the change to form from circumstance.
For how could one exist without a shadow? how
could the other create a relative world with a rod of
  singularity?
One was the necessary god of wrath and proclamation.
He was the one who Did Things.
He brooded over the cosmos like a slack
mouth, laughed and cried a lot being given to whims
and to polarities. It was He who conceived of mirrors
in a moment bound by the ordinance of time.

How pleased He must have been with His engendered world.
How He must have acted upon each reaction, each Vesuvial
burst of new configurations coming to His created senses
(for these He must create too in order to appreciate Himself)
with the compunction of beginnings, the terror of ellipses
as what had been begun began to grow
and take upon itself its own begetting.

The other god, the silent one, the one for whom seas
and lava flows were things of little consequence folded
in upon Herself vulvally (being more intent on being
than on doing something), and so has hidden from us
in the permanent void that runs between accessible
worlds like the lines on a blank sheet of paper.
She is not His opposite, God the Father
or His begotten Son. She will not come when prophets call.
Only in secrets—the climax, the womb,
the folds of flesh between thighs, the armpits,
the pits of fruit and innocence—can She be found.

And then there's only the primal scent of Her to smell,
accompanied by a whirling backwards through small holes
of tonal opposition—a kind of prehistoric musical pause.
Unlike any mathematical encounter with machines, this un-
sound stems from the flesh; it is the sound our voices
once made; it is all She is and all that we can be.
It does not say, "Thou shalt love the Lord thy God"
for might is an irrelevance. It does not bluster or buffoon,
crave or misbehave, cajole, command, or pester.

Until we decipher the giants of the sea, whale song
may be the closest sound we have to it:
a suspended echoing of some unknown against
another sent through mediums where we don't belong
by creatures we can never know. Soon,
when scientists tell us, "This tone = that desire,"
whale song will not work as metaphor.

Dissolving into the rudeness of the alphabet,
the sign will fade like a bleached flag. We shall go back
to brass bands and court injunctions, listen again
for the meanings of the stars, shuttle off
to spheres we sweat upon and measure,
take stock, play with numbers
like a rogue abacus, believing light is quantifiable,
death a word for reaching up and not for reaching in.

On Seeing Things

The sky is green, the grass is blue
with cold, and words take place
before the sound is done.
I cannot write.
The earth is layered with bones
and soldier ants are waiting for the signal to attack.
The sky is shot with ripening
as complementary reds begin their bloodlines
round the shapely clouds.

The sky cannot be green, you know,
my six-year-old declares. *It's blue
because I sawn it.* I have sawn it too.
With sharp instruments I've beheaded
and dissected whatever I've held close.
I'm a writer; that's my job.

But I would love, for once, to only sense the subject
without sensing that I'm doing so.
I want to see without seeing how I've seen,
to hear without listening to the sound
of my translation. The sorrow is always
words—and the fact that there is nothing
in between to comfort them.

The sky is green, the earth is blue
with cold. I cannot see without a sig-
nature. The alphabet of loss is still
the alphabet.

Gospel

When she sang like a woman washing her hands,
we sat back in our pews and let the hard brown wood
polish us to common brightness.

When she sang like a woman torn by sickle moons
we rode our pews like horses—
our breath short, our mouths puckered
into small stars.

We sang with her, leaning forward into the kiss.
Her sharps and flats, the fat roll
of her crescendoes cradled us.
Yes! Yes! we say, as bliss hits us
broadside and flings us into faith.
The voice maroons itself; we have to go
and fetch it—carry it back home across the sea.
Nobody knows anything but the voice
on the island, telling us to remember how stairs
are built into the sky; how fast you must row
when the sea is kind; how rarely
you must listen out over the bow
for bones; how often
you must answer her in the contrapuntal
caves of song.

All of us are tired.
But the woman's voice stands up
as straight as the hair on our heads
and claps for us.
A sudden surfacing of wings:
a great black hand skimming light from the sea;

gulls wheeling high up in the air
where her voice is—
on the top stair
like something newly crowned
rolling up its sleeves.

About the Author

LUCINDA ROY has received the Felix Christopher McKean
Award for poetry from the University of Arkansas; the
Madeline Sadin Award for poetry from *New York Quarterly/
Pulpsmith*; and the Baxter Hathaway Poetry Prize from *Epoch*,
Cornell University. Her work has appeared in *Callaloo*,
Shenandoah, *The American Poetry Review*, *Oxford Magazine*, *The
New Orleans Review*, *The Greensboro Review*, *Negative Capability*,
and *The Denver Quarterly*, among others. She grew up in
London, the daughter of a British mother and a Jamaican
father. She received her undergraduate education at King's
College, London, and her M.F.A. at the University of
Arkansas. She is currently an associate dean at Virginia Tech
in Blacksburg, Virginia, where she is also the Gloria D. Smith
Professor of English and Black Studies. Her first book of
poetry, *Wailing the Dead to Sleep*, was published in Great
Britain in 1988 by Bogle L'Ouverture. She is a visual artist as
well as a writer and academician. She is working on series of
oil paintings about the Middle Passage. *Suffering the Sea
Change: Not Venus, but Rising*, reproduced on the cover of *The
Humming Birds*, is part of this series.

poetry

TRYING TO BE AN HONEST WOMAN
Judith Barrington
$6.95

HISTORY AND GEOGRAPHY
Judith Barrington
$7.95

A FEW WORDS IN THE MOTHER TONGUE
POEMS SELECTED AND NEW (1971–1990)
Irena Klepfisz
Introduction by Adrienne Rich
$11.95

SEVEN HANDS, SEVEN HEARTS
Elizabeth Woody
$13.95

WORDS UNDER THE WORDS
Naomi Shihab Nye
$13.95

fiction

THE RIVERHOUSE STORIES
Andrea Carlisle
$8.95

INCIDENTS INVOLVING MIRTH
Anna Livia
$9.95

MINIMAX
Anna Livia
$9.95

COWS AND HORSES
Barbara Wilson
$9.95

essays

DREAMS OF AN INSOMNIAC
JEWISH FEMINIST ESSAYS, SPEECHES, AND DIATRIBES
Irena Klepfisz
Introduction by Evelyn Torton Beck
$11.95

EVERYDAY ACTS AND SMALL SUBVERSIONS
WOMEN REINVENTING FAMILY, COMMUNITY, AND HOME
Anndee Hochman
$12.95

AN INTIMATE WILDERNESS
LESBIAN WRITERS ON SEXUALITY
Judith Barrington, Editor
$14.95

travel

A JOURNEY OF ONE'S OWN
UNCOMMON ADVICE FOR
THE INDEPENDENT WOMAN TRAVELER
Thalia Zepatos
$16.95

ADVENTURES IN GOOD COMPANY
THE COMPLETE GUIDE TO
WOMEN'S TOURS AND OUTDOOR TRIPS
Thalia Zepatos
$16.95

THE FEARLESS FLYER
HOW TO FLY IN COMFORT
AND WITHOUT TREPIDATION
Cherry Hartman and Julie Sheldon Huffaker
$10.95

To order a book directly from the Eighth Mountain Press, send a check for the
total of the book order, plus $2.50 postage and handling for the first book, (50¢
for each additional book) to 624 Southeast 29th Avenue, Portland, Oregon 97214.
Books will be mailed "book rate." For faster delivery or for any questions call
503/233-3936 or fax us at 503/233-0774.